A BEACON BIOGRAPHY

Harry
STYLES
of
One Direction

Heidi
Krumenauer

PURPLE TOAD
PUBLISHING

P.O. Box 631
Kennett Square, Pennsylvania 19348
www.purpletoadpublishing.com

Printing   1   2   3   4   5   6   7   8   9

A Beacon Biography

Big Time Rush
Carly Rae Jepsen
Drake
Harry Styles of One Direction
Jennifer Lawrence
Kevin Durant
Robert Griffin III (RG3)

Publisher's Cataloging-in-Publication Data
Krumenauer, Heidi
  Harry Styles / Heidi Krumenauer
    p. cm. – (A beacon biography)
Includes bibliographic references and index.
ISBN: 978-1-62469-008-2 (library bound)
1. Styles, Harry, 1994–. 2. One Direction (Musical group) – Juvenile literature. 3. Singers – Great Britain – Biography – Juvenile literature.   I. Title.
ML3930.O66K78 2013
782.4216'4092 – dc23

                                      2013930986

eBook ISBN: 978-1-62469-019-8

ABOUT THE AUTHOR: Heidi Krumenauer has written more than 1,200 newspaper and magazine articles. She has contributed chapters to 17 nonfiction book projects, including several for the *Chicken Soup for the Soul* series. Her first book, *Why Does Grandma Have a Wibble?*, was released in 2007. She has also written several youth biographies: *Brett Favre, Rihanna, Sean Kingston, Joe Flacco, Lady Gaga, Flo Rida, Jimmie Johnson,* and *Michael Strahan.* Krumenauer is a 1991 graduate of the University of Wisconsin–Platteville. She is in upper management with a Fortune 400 insurance company. She and her husband, Jeff, raise their sons, Noah and Payton, in Southern Wisconsin.

PUBLISHER'S NOTE: The data in this book has been researched in depth, and to the best of our knowledge is factual. Although every measure is taken to give an accurate account, Purple Toad Publishing makes no warranty of the accuracy of the information and is not liable for damages caused by inaccuracies. This story has not been authorized or endorsed by Harry Styles.

Printed by Lake Book Manufacturing, Chicago, IL

CONTENTS

Harry Styles wows the judges when he sings Stevie Wonder's "Isn't She Lovely" on *The X Factor* on September 19, 2010.

Harry Has The X Factor

After his mother kissed his cheek and his family wished him well, sixteen-year-old Harry Styles took his place on *The X Factor* stage in Manchester, England, during the summer of 2010. The episode aired on September 19, 2010. The popular television show began in the United Kingdom (UK) as a way to find extraordinary talent and launch the careers of a select group of people who dreamed of finding fame.

Harry was convinced he had something special, and he hoped the judges (Simon Cowell, Nicole Scherzinger, and Louis Walsh) would agree. "I've always wanted to do it, and my mum's always wanted me to do it, but I haven't been old enough. I thought I'd give it a whirl," he told *The X Factor* crew before his audition. "I'm quite nervous, but I'm quite excited because when I get told I'm good, it's by my friends or my family, so I want to find out from someone who knows what they're talking about. If I was to get through, it would be just like everything . . . It's everything I want to do. If the people [who] can make that happen for me don't think I should be doing that, then it's a major setback in my plans," he said.

In high school, Harry worked at the W. Mandeville Bakery. He served bakery goods, scrubbed the floor, washed the trays and cleaned the counter.

Before Harry sang for the judges, Simon wanted to know something about his life. "I work in a bakery. I work there on Saturdays. I'm going to college in September." Of course, Simon wanted to know what he would study. "Law. Sociology. Business. And something else, but I'm not sure yet," Harry said.

After performing Stevie Wonder's "Isn't She Lovely" for the judges, Harry found the judges to be divided in whether or not they wanted him to move on to the next round. Nicole told him, "I'm really glad we had the opportunity to hear you sing a capella. We could really hear how great your voice is. For sixteen years old, you have a beautiful voice." Louis agreed with Nicole, but added, "I think you're so young, I don't think you have enough experience or confidence yet. For all the right reasons, I'm going to say no as I don't think you're ready."

Simon wasn't happy with Louis's vote. "Someone in the audience just said 'rubbish,' and I totally agree with them. The show is designed to find someone like you; whether you're sixteen, seventeen, it doesn't matter. I think with a bit of vocal coaching you actually could be very good," Simon told Harry.

Nicole placed her vote by saying, "I like you, Harry. I'm going to say yes!" Simon's vote came next. "And you'll be happy to hear that I'm going to be agreeing with Nicole," he said. "You're through to the next round." With two yes votes, Harry won a spot in *The X Factor* boot camp!

And to think that Harry's audition on *The X Factor* stage almost didn't happen. He began vomiting and coughing up blood shortly before he was supposed to go on stage. He was so sick, his parents rushed him to the hospital. "I remember I kept throwing up, and then I got really bad and I started coughing up blood," he told *Now Daily*. Luckily, he was released from the hospital in time for the audition. "They discharged me, but to this day I don't know what it was."

Harry's mother Anne Cox and her husband Robin Twist nervously watched Harry's X Factor *auditions.*

Harry grew up and attended school in Holmes Chapel, Cheshire, England, a village of less than 6,000 residents.

Life Before One Direction

Harry Edward Styles was born on February 1, 1994, to Anne Cox and Des Styles. He has one older sister, Gemma. Harry grew up in Holmes Chapel, Cheshire, England. "It's quite boring. There's nothing much happens there. It's quite picturesque," says Harry of his hometown.

Harry's parents divorced when he was seven years old. "That was quite a weird time," Harry recalls in the band's book, *Dare to Dream: Life as One Direction*. "I remember crying about it. I didn't really get what was going on properly. I was just sad that my parents wouldn't be together anymore. My mum, my older sister Gemma, and I left Holmes Chapel and moved further out into the Cheshire countryside." His new home was a pub where his mother became the landlady. Even though his parents were divorced, Harry maintained a good relationship with both of them. "I'm such a momma's boy. I'm really close to my dad as well, and he's very supportive of everything I'm doing. I think we're probably quite alike in a lot of ways," Harry said. Harry's dad influenced him with his favorite music when he was young. "I used to love singing. The first song I knew all the words to was

Harry and his father, Des

'Girl of My Best Friend' by Elvis. When I got given a karaoke machine by my granddad, my cousin and I recorded a load of Elvis tracks," he says in his book.

Harry attended Holmes Chapel Comprehensive School, and while there, he could often be found on stage performing in plays. His first performance was the role of Buzz Lightyear in *Chitty Chitty Bang Bang*. Buzz was one of the toys in the toy shop where the children were hiding. Later, when he performed in the play *Barney*, Harry dressed up in his sister's gray tights and headband with ears and sang in front of the audience as a mouse. "I like to think I was a good mouse," Harry joked.

Academically, Harry enjoyed math early on, but as he got older, he preferred English classes because he was a good writer and he was proud of his work. He found it difficult to concentrate on his studies, though, because he loved people and focused more on talking with them. "I was so easily distracted that I started spending more and more time chatting to friends in class or daydreaming."

Young Harry

Harry enjoys some family time with his mother and stepfather, Robin.

Being a social guy made it easy for Harry to fit into a team environment. He took an interest in soccer and played on the local team where he made a lot of friends from his school and neighboring schools. He also enjoyed playing badminton, a sport that he learned from his dad.

When Harry was twelve years old, his family moved back to Holmes Chapel. That's when Harry's mother, Anne, met and started dating Robin Twist. Anne wanted her kids to be comfortable with Robin around, but that was never a problem for Harry. He liked Robin, and would even text to invite him over to spend time with the family. "I was really pleased when Robin proposed to my mum," Harry said.

Harry's first band, White Eskimo, is an alternative pop/rock band that continues to entertain audiences.

At the end of Harry's eighth year of school, he met Will Sweeny, Haydn Morris, and Nick Clough. The boys wanted to enter a Battle of the Bands competition at their school, so they asked Harry to try out as the singer. "That was a bit of a shock for me as I'd only ever sung to myself in the shower or the car," Harry said. As the band started to take shape, they needed a name. Harry randomly chose the name *White Eskimo,* and the guys liked it. For the battle of the bands, the group sang "Summer of '69" by Bryan Adams in the school lunchroom. White Eskimo won the competition! After that, they practiced every Wednesday after school, hoping to get better and land a real job performing in front of others. Their first gig was at a wedding where they performed 25 songs. "We got paid £160 [about US $260] for the gig, and we got sandwiches. What more can you ask for?" Harry says in *Dare to Dream*.

Deep down, Harry did want more!

As the lead singer of White Eskimo, Harry sang his heart out for his school's Battle of the Bands competition and it worked. They won!

One Direction got their start on *The X Factor* Britain stage in 2010. Two years later, their popularity put them back on the stage at *The X Factor* USA finals.

As the boys progressed through each round, the judges came to a conclusion. They decided that the boys would have more success competing as a group rather than as individual singers. So, instead of cutting the boys from the competition, the judges grouped Harry and the other boys together into a boy band. In the summer of 2010, Harry auditioned before the judges and passed through to the next round. So did Niall Horan, Zayn Malik, Liam Payne, and Louis Tomlinson. As the boys moved through the competitive rounds, it became apparent to the judges that they were good as individuals, but felt they would have more talent as a group. Rather than being dismissed from the competition, the judges grouped Harry and the other boys together to see if forming a boy band might work. Guest judge and Pussycat Dolls singer Nicole Scherzinger told the boys, "We thought you were too talented to let go."

"The minute they stood there for the first time together—it was a weird feeling. They just looked like a group at that point," Simon Cowell told *Rolling Stone* magazine. "I had a good feeling, but then obviously we had about a five-week wait where they had to work together. They had to come back for another section of the show where they performed together as a group for the first time. I was concerned whether five weeks was long enough, but they came back five weeks later and were absolutely sensational." During those weeks, the boys stayed at Harry's stepfather's home, bonding, hanging out, getting to know each other's personalities, and above all, practicing.

When the group came back to compete against the other final 32 acts in the competition, they had a new name: One Direction. Their goal was to win the competition and a recording contract. On December 11, 2010, One Direction learned their fate after singing Natalie Imbruglia's "Torn" for a public vote. They were voted off the show and left with only third place.

Harry was upset with the results. "I cried as soon as we got off stage, and then I stopped, took some deep breaths and was fine again," he says in *Dare to Dream*. Simon wasn't happy either. "I'm absolutely gutted," he told *The X Factor* host Dermot O'Leary. Simon knew it wasn't the end of the road for the band. "This is just the beginning for these boys," he said. And he was right.

One Direction spends time in recording studios around the world, like Ireland, England, and the United States.

The X Factor's Simon Cowell has always supported One Direction. "The more I got to know them, the more I liked them and the more I trusted them," he told Rolling Stone *magazine.*

The next day, Simon called the band to his office to offer One Direction a record deal. Harry cried again, but this time it was tears of joy. "As soon as Simon told us we had a record deal, I started crying again and I sat there thinking, 'Why am I crying? If this works out it's going to totally change my life.' It's one of those things you always want to hear, and then when you hear it you don't know how to react."

There was little time to bask in the glory of a record deal. Harry and his friends had work to do in preparing songs for their first album. In January 2011, the group began recording songs for the album *Up All Night*, which was released by Syco Music in November 2011 in Ireland and the United Kingdom. The album was released in the United States on March 13, one week earlier than planned due to high fan demand. One Direction's first single, "What Makes You Beautiful," was a number one hit in Britain and Ireland. It went to number four on Billboard's singles chart after its release in the United States.

Harry's curly locks and often-copied style come with a lot of work. Harry revealed that he uses hair products to get his famous windblown look.

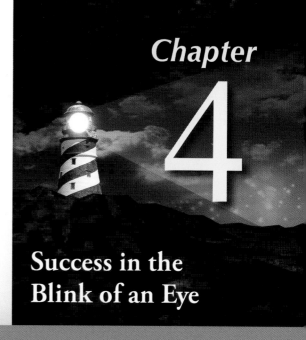

Success in the Blink of an Eye

Harry's rise to fame happened in such a short time, it's no wonder everyone wants to know how this is affecting him. Larry London of *Voice of America* (VOA) talked to Harry in March 2012 about his new life. Harry replied, "We're normal teenage guys so for all this to be happening is absolutely crazy. And we're having so much fun. We work so, so hard, so we play hard as well."

It's hard to be a normal teenager, though, when others are comparing One Direction to The Beatles. "I think if you base your career on trying to achieve someone else's goals, that's kind of the wrong way to do it," Harry told London. "So, it's incredibly flattering. I'm a massive fan of the Beatles. I listened to them growing up. So to have that comparison is huge, but, at the same time, we kind of find it a bit ridiculous because the Beatles are such an icon."

So how does an eighteen-year-old celebrate new success? Harry decided that above anything else, he would buy a new mattress. "I'm going to treat myself to a new one. The one I'm using is still the one that was there when I moved in. The springs have gone," he told *The Sun*. "I hear those memory foam ones are good. I need one of those."

Harry splurged a little more than that, according to *Mail Online*. While his friends were purchasing expensive homes in the millions, Harry watched his budget a bit more and spent £575,000 (or about US $925,000) for an East London property.

In the spring of 2012, One Direction toured Australia and the United States where every show was sold out. When the band performed for the *Today* show on the streets of New York City on March 11, about 15,000 attended the free concert. That was a *Today* show record!

During an interview on Nick Grimshaw's radio show, Harry noted that one of his highlights was performing on *Saturday Night Live (SNL)*. In March 2012, he told June Simms of *VOA* that the band has had many great experiences in their travels, but one

One Direction performs "One Thing" on SNL during a trip to New York in April 2012.

Harry and his bandmates entertain a large crowd at Madison Square Garden in New York City in April 2012.

of his most exciting events was playing at Madison Square Garden in New York City. "It's such a prestigious venue. To be playing there is a great honor," Harry said.

Maybe an even greater honor happened on August 12, 2012, when Harry and his One Direction pals sang "What Makes You Beautiful" at the Olympics Closing Ceremony in London. An estimated four billion people tuned in to watch the event.

One Direction's worldwide recognition will, no doubt, make the release of their second album an even greater success. In August 2012, the band announced that *Take Me Home* would be released on November 13 that year.

Is the second album going to be like the first one? Harry told Larry London: "I think it's important that we don't try too many new things too soon. I think that sound is very us so I think it's gonna be the same kind of vibe as the first album. I think the music will grow up as we grow up."

Harry was voted the 18th hottest hunk of 2012 by the readers of *Heat* magazine, beating out Brad Pitt and Justin Timberlake.

Just when the boys appeared to have done it all, Harry and his band mates were scheduled to be turned into comic book characters for the magazine *Fame: One Direction.* The comic book adventure would feature the band's exciting first eighteen months as they quickly rose to

One Direction's second album, *Take Me Home*

fame. Harry is a video game celebrity, too. He and the rest of One Direction star in *Pokémon Black* and *Pokémon White* for Nintendo DS and Nintendo DSi.

The honors just keep coming for Harry and his band-mates. One Direction was a featured act at the 2012 MTV Video Music Awards in Los Angeles. Girls went crazy for One Direction as they performed "One Thing." They also brought home two of the famous MTV Moonman trophies for Best Pop Video and Most-Share Worthy Video for "What Makes You Beautiful." They grabbed another trophy for Best New Artist. When pop singer Katy Perry presented the trophy for Best Pop Video, she made sure to get a kiss—on the lips—from Niall and Harry. Twitter posts lit up all over the country as One Direction's fans expressed their jealousy. Harry did his own tweeting to thank his fans for their support: "We owe you everything. Thank you so much for this. Three *VMAs*!! YEAH!"

One Direction (left to right): Harry Styles, Liam Payne, Louis Tomlinson, Niall Horan, and Zayn Malik

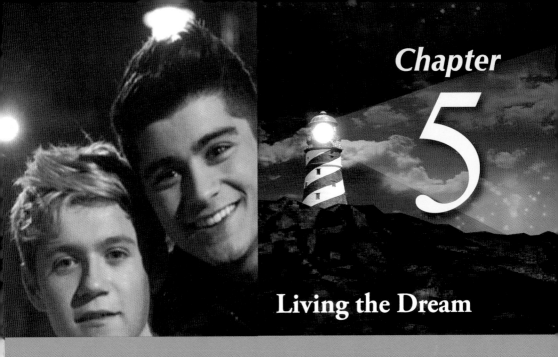

Before One Direction, Harry spent his Saturdays at W. Mandeville bakery in Holmes Chapel, but he wasn't ordering pastries. He was working there, trying to make a few dollars. "He is a great lad and was really popular with the customers when he used to work on counter," said bakery owner Simon Wakefield. "He's welcome back any time, but I highly doubt he'll be back to work."

While a job at a bakery might not live up to the fame and income that Harry enjoys now, he admits he often misses the normal routine. "There are times I would like to go home and see my old friends again and go to all of the old places," he says in *Dare to Dream*.

With his new friends, though, life on the road is an adventure. Harry says the worst part of traveling with his pals is that if he falls asleep, the band will prank him by drawing on his face. But that doesn't upset him. "The best thing is that you get to travel around with four of your best friends doing what you love to do," he told *Heat* magazine in October 2011. In *Dare to Dream*, Harry talks about how close he has become to his four friends of

One Direction. "We've become better friends than I could ever have imagined and it's so nice to have four other guys to share this experience with. I think we're going to get tighter and tighter as time goes on," he says.

Harry's time on the road and friendship with his buddies isn't the only thing that's important to him. An eleven-year-old boy named Harry Moseley was sick from a brain tumor, and so was his friend, Robert. Moseley decided to make bracelets to sell. These would raise money and awareness for brain cancer research. Although Moseley died from his tumor in October 2011, his charity, Help Harry Help Others, is still thriving. Harry Styles was proud to support the charity and told *BOP* and *Tiger Beat* in February 2012, "Please help us keep his dream alive by wearing one of his bracelets in memory of a very special Harry."

Harry Moseley, an eleven-year-old boy with brain cancer, sold bracelets to raise money for the disease. Harry Styles proudly supported the young man—with the same name—by wearing some of his own.

That's not the only time Harry wore a bracelet to raise money. For months, he was photographed wearing a purple bracelet to raise awareness for Believe in Magic, a charity that provides seriously and terminally ill children with "special and once-in-a-lifetime experiences." Harry's signed bracelet was auctioned on eBay in May 2012 for more than £2,150 (US $3,400).

Harry, along with his One Direction band mates, has also publicly supported Sport Relief, Comic Relief, and Greenpeace.

At the end of the day, Harry is a teenager who enjoys the simple things of life —like sweet corn, apple juice, and the television show *Family Guy*. He knows how to juggle. He loves massages and going out for dinner with his friends. And if he could choose the perfect day, Harry would take a nap and relax.

There hasn't been a lot of time to relax, though. With a 2013 World Tour scheduled, more songs to record, and millions of fans to please, Harry would be moving in his own one direction for a very long time—the direction of success!

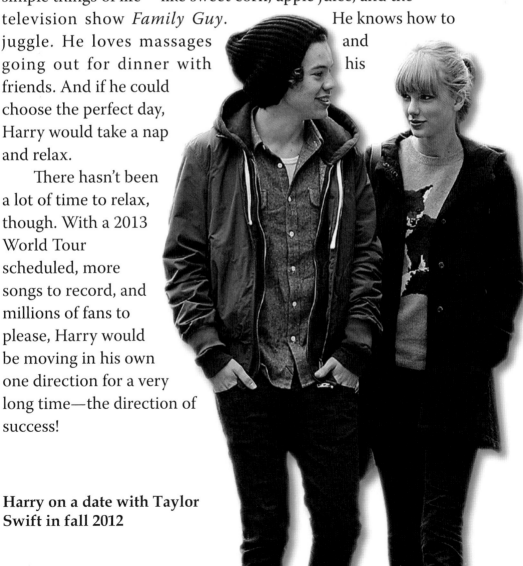

Harry on a date with Taylor Swift in fall 2012

1994 Harry Edward Styles is born to Anne Cox and Des Styles in Holmes Chapel, Cheshire, England.

2001 Anne and Des divorce.

2010 White Eskimo, Harry's first band, wins a high school Battle of the Bands competition. Harry auditions for *The X Factor*. On July 23, One Direction is formed at the request of *The X Factor* judges Simon Cowell, Nicole Scherzinger, and Louis Walsh, who felt Harry and four other solo singers were too talented to be sent home. On December 11, One Direction leaves the competition with third place. The next day, Simon Cowell offers the band a recording contract.

2011 In January, One Direction begins recording *Up All Night*. The album is released in Ireland and the UK in November. The single "What Makes You Beautiful" becomes a hit.

2012 On March 21 in the United States, *Up All Night* enters the Billboard 200 pop album chart at #1, the first time ever for a debut album by a UK band. The band performs at the Olympics closing ceremony in London on August 12. One Direction takes home three awards at MTV's Video Music Award Show on September 6. The band releases their second album, *Take Me Home*, on November 13. One Direction plans for second world tour in 2013. One Direction appears on the Today Show to celebrate the album's release. In November, Harry and singing superstar Taylor Swift reveal they are dating. One Direction is selected as one of the "10 Most Fascinating People" by Barbara Walters, who interviews the band in December.

2013 One Direction's World Tour kicks off in Europe in February. The band continues touring North America and Australia through October.

DISCOGRAPHY

Albums

2012   **Take Me Home**

2011   **Up All Night**

Hit Singles

"What Makes You Beautiful"

"One Thing"

"Up All Night"

Books

Boone, Mary. *One Direction: What Makes You Beautiful.* Chicago: Triumph Books, 2012.

One Direction. *Dare to Dream: Life as One Direction.* Hammersmith, London: HarperCollins UK, 2012.

One Direction. *One Direction: Behind the Scenes.* Hammersmith, London: HarperCollins, 2012.

One Direction. *One Direction: Forever Young: Our Official X Factor Story.* Hammersmith, London: HarperCollins, 2011.

Works Consulted

Greene, Andy. "Exclusive Q&A: Simon Cowell on One Direction's Rise to Stardom." *Rolling Stone.* April 9, 2012. http://www.rollingstone.com/music/news/exclusive-q-a-simon-cowell-on-one-directions-rise-to-stardom-20120409#ixzz25H4LxLnV

Halewood, Simon. "Holmes Chapel Bakery Backs X Factor Star Harry Styles." *Crewe Chronicle.* October 22, 2010. http://www.crewechronicle.co.uk/crewe-news/harry-styles-x-factor-one-direction/2010/10/22/holmes-chapel-bakery-backs-rising-x-factor-star-harry-styles-96135-27519328/

"Harry Styles Has Got the X Factor in Holmes Chapel." *BBC News.* November 17, 2010. http://news.bbc.co.uk/local/stoke/hi/people_and_places/music/newsid_9195000/9195671.stm

"Harry Styles Helps Another Harry—For a Great Cause." *Bop and Tiger Beat.* February 13, 2012. http://www.bopandtigerbeat.com/2012/02/harry-styles-helps-another-harry-—%C2%A0for-a-great-cause/

"Harry Styles Nearly Missed X Factor Audition." *Entertainment STV.* December 30, 2011. http://entertainment.stv.tv/tv/291901-harry-styles-nearly-missed-x-factor-audition/

"Harry Styles of One Direction: 'We Work So, So Hard and Play Hard as Well.'" *VOANews.com.* May 31, 2012. http://learningenglish.voanews.com/content/one-direction-harry-styles-youthwork-homeless/1145890.html

"Harry Styles to Celebrate American Success with a New Mattress." *Sugarscape.* March 23, 2012. http://www.sugarscape.com/main-topics/lads/706025/harry-styles-celebrate-american-success-new-mattress

"Harry Styles' Believe In Magic Charity Wristband Fetches Thousands as It Goes Up for Auction." *Now Daily.* May 21, 2012. http://www.nowmagazine.co.uk/celebrity-news/536332/one-direction-star-harry-styles-believe-in-magic-charity-wristband-fetches-thousands-as-it-goes-up-for-auction

Jill, Jodi. "Harry Styles Says Fans Are Reason for Big VMA Wins: 'We Owe You Everything.' " *Examiner.* September 6, 2012. http://www.examiner.com/article/harry-styles-says-fans-are-reason-for-big-vma-wins-we-owe-you-everything

Look to the Stars. "One Direction." http://www.looktothestars.org/celebrity/2850-one-direction

McCormack, Kirsty. "Simon Cowell Will Be Pleased! One Direction Set to Be Worth £64 Million This Time Next Year." *Mail Online.* June 16, 2012. http://www.

dailymail.co.uk/tvshowbiz/article-2160187/One-Direction-set-worth-64million-time-year.html

McGarry, Lisa. "X Factor 2010: Simon Cowell Tells Harry Styles, 'This Show Is Designed to Find Someone Like You.'" *Unreality TV.* September 19, 2010. http://www.unrealitytv.co.uk/x-factor/x-factor-2010-simon-cowell-tells-harry-styles-this-show-is-designed-to-find-someone-like-you-video/

Mansfield, Brian. "Meet U.K. Boy Band One Direction." *USAToday.* March 7, 2012. http://www.usatoday.com/life/music/ontheverge/story/2012-03-07/one-direction/53425236/1

"One Direction Announce Date for Second Album Release." *TVNZ.co.nz.* August 31, 2012. http://tvnz.co.nz/entertainment-news/one-direction-announce-date-second-album-release-5054011?ref=emailfriend

One Direction. *Dare to Dream: Life as One Direction.* HarperCollins UK. September 15, 2011.

Robertson, James. "Watch One Direction's Amazing Olympics Closing Ceremony Performance." *Mirror Online.* August 12, 2012. http://www.mirror.co.uk/3am/celebrity-news/video-one-direction-closing-ceremony-1256743

Ryan, Belinda. "Holmes Chapel X Factor Star Harry Styles Can Win Show Say School Bandmates." *Crewe Chronicle.* September 29, 2010. http://www.crewechronicle.co.uk/crewe-news/local-crewe-news/2010/09/29/holmes-chapel-x-factor-star-harry-styles-can-win-show-say-school-bandmates-96135-27359480/

Saunders, Louise. "Gotta Be You: One Direction Are Immortalized in Cartoon Form in a New Comic Book which Charts Their Rise to Fame." *Mail Online.* August 30, 2012. http://www.dailymail.co.uk/tvshowbiz/article-2196011/One-Direction-immortalised-cartoon-form-new-comic-book-charts-rise-fame.html#ixzz25H6EMsOF

"X Factor Final: One Direction Booted Off, Rebecca and Matt Left." *Metro.* December 12, 2010. http://www.metro.co.uk/tv/850216-x-factor-final-one-direction-booted-off-rebecca-and-matt-left

On the Internet

Billboard, One Direction. http://www.billboard.com/artist/one-direction/1748710#/artist/one-direction/1748710

Harry Styles, One Direction, Answers Twitter Questions. October 4, 2011. http://www.youtube.com/watch?v=e2CkIbuJjoU

Harry Styles-On Why He Auditioned for The X-Factor. March 17, 2012. http://www.youtube.com/watch?v=lHYaWneNz20

Harry Styles X-Factor Auditon. September 19, 2010. http://www.youtube.com/watch?v=irKluYOMkI0&feature=em-share_video_user&noredirect=1

Help Harry Help Others. http://hhho.org.uk/

One Direction News (MTV). http://www.mtv.com/artists/one-direction/

One Direction Official Site. http://www.onedirectionmusic.com/us/

a capella: To sing without instrumental accompaniment.

Auto-Tune: The trademark for an audio processor created by Antares Audio Technologies that automatically corrects musical pitch.

comprehensive school: A British public high school.

debut: A first public appearance on a stage, on television, and the like.

landlady: As used in the United Kingdom, this term refers to a woman's job at a pub.

picturesque: Charming in a visual sense.

rubbish: Garbage (as used in the United Kingdom).

venue: The place or location of an event.

A very young Harry

INDEX